DEDICATION

This book is dedicated with love and gratitude to
My parents, Mr. and Mrs. Mbong J. Mbong,
for teaching me never to give up in life.

To order additional copies of this book, contact:
Xlibris
844-714-8691
www.Xlibris.com
Orders@Xlibris.com

ISBN: Softcover   978-1-4363-5335-9
           EBook   978-1-6641-8477-0

Print information available on the last page

Rev. date: 07/12/2021

You Have What It Takes

Grace J. Mbong

ACKNOWLEDGMENTS

First and foremost, I dedicate this book to my Lord and Savior Jesus Christ. Without him bestowing the gift on me, I would never have picked up a pen to write. I thank God for the insights and the ability he gave me for writing.

To my Mum. Thank you for always encouraging me to work hard for the things I want and believe in while on this journey called life. Thank you for all your prayers.

To my Dad. You are one of my main supporters, and I love you. Thank you for your love and support. You have aided in providing me with the spiritual growth and direction I needed. You are my inspiration.

To my siblings, Emmanuel and Joy. Thank you so much for the courage and strength you have given me. I love you. Gloria Bassey, thank you so much for your love and support.

Thank you to my mentors, Pastor Tony and Sherry Stallings. You have provided me with great strength. Your words of inspirations each day will always be treasured. Alabaster Choir Of Highest Praise Church of God, thank you so much for your love and encouragements, always listening to my poetry. I would not have made this without you. I love you all.

To the following friends: Esther Etuk, Paulette Wright, Mary Adoga, Aniefiok Inyang, Pastor Moses Saquee, Gubrilla Dumbuya, Iyabo Mokunye, Theresa Morrison, Avis Hannah, Theresa Barnett (African queen), Clyde Holmes, Chris Roberts, Ratana Landry, Put two (queen of the house), Querie Orr, Emma and Bassey Duke, Okpon Akpan, Eme Udi (Big sister), Usoro Itata, Eliza Sillas, Martine Babilla and Eugena Jones. Thanks also to Esin/Sunny Abia, Chief Usua Amanam, Eket Community and Akwa Ibom State Association of America, Pastor Raphael Grant and Pastor Ime Ibanga and the rest of my friends to mention a few. Thank you so much for believing in me.

To my very good friends who has taken me under their wings and opened doors for me with their unconditional love, Mariama and Osman Sesay. Thank you so much for your love, encouragement, and most of all believing in me as a friend. I love you with all my heart.

To my publisher, Xlibris. Thank you for all your help.

From Zero to a Hero

I can remember images of myself as a little girl. Sometimes I was not the prettiest in the group at least in all eyes. I was mocked and made fun of because of a disfiguration in my face. Somehow, through all my childhood years, I tried to do things and of no good result. Struggling and all doors getting shut, I always believed that one day, I will excel to the top. I have been put together by my parents who encouraged me and my best friends Mariama and Osman Sesay who accepted me for who I am.

If I had let the views of others direct this book, I would never have made it to this place and time. A place where I recognize that I can do all things through Christ who strengthens me. The hidden treasures and endless potentials are buried beneath the initiative and launch into action. This book is designed to challenge you and ignite your faith to encourage you and show you to take the action needed to fulfill your destiny. It will also unlock the treasure of potential, power, and purpose that resides in you.

CONTENTS

BELIEVE IN YOURSELF

We are surrounded by many words about ourselves
Words of inspirations, hopes, and discouragements
Opportunities to think, feel, and learn
Wisdom to know what is right or wrong

What can I say about myself?
Of what use am I in this world we are living
Whatever you do, you will reap at the end
Strive hard with motivation and believe in yourself.

YOU HAVE WHAT IT TAKES

You have what it takes to make it
You are beautiful and blessed
Talented in different ways
In everything you do

You are strong as a brick
Nothing can stop you
Nothing can shake you off
Because you have the power of God in you

The power of God is all around you
His presence is always with you
Do not fear for anything
You have what it takes to make it

YOU ARE MY ROCK

You are the rope I hold on to each day
The sound of your voice keeps a smile on your face
The strength I have I drew it from you
For you alone has touched the deepest part of my heart.

You are a great and mighty God
My deliverer, peace, and my provision
No one else deserves all my praise
You are my joy, my all in all.

STRESS, A SERIAL KILLER

It kills the soul, it breaks the heart
It brings frustration to you every day
This makes you think that there is no God
Why stress it out when God is with you

I have no hope, no one to turn to
This stress is serious, it needs medical attention
Nobody can help you out with your stress
You have to let this disease die out from you

Take control of yourself, if you don't, you might die
Relax and never let stress take your joy from you
Put on a smiling face and don't spoil the day
Give your stress to God and he will ease the pain.

YOU DESERVE MY PRAISE

No man on earth deserves this royalty
No one is entitled to this honor
You are the one who did it all for me
When I did not have any help
Thank you, God, for everything you have done
You deserve my praise.

DON T SETTLE FOR LESS

Nothing in life comes as a surprise
It takes determination and patience to get there
The road to success is not an easy road
It looks narrow, difficult but needs persistence

Let no one tell you that you are a loser
Sometimes it takes time for your dream to manifest
Do not settle for less and think it is all over
You can make it if you really want to in life

DROP THE VEIL

Things happen in our lives that we need God
To protect, guide, and settle our problems
We seek and yearn when things get out of control
We smile when we hear the gospel of Jesus
And harden our hearts and look the other way

When fame, money takes a hold of us all
Sometimes we remember but it takes a while to reverence God
But often we neglect and show a lot of pride
Bragging, screaming, "I accomplished all this by myself"
Neglecting to say, "Thank you, God, for my success"

Remember, it is God that gave you power to make wealth
He is the giver of all the provisions in life
Be careful of what you say, God is watching you
Take heed in life lest you fall
Take off the veil and get closer to God

EMERGENCY WIG 911

Walking outside on a cold winter day
The day is cold, the breeze is blowing
The trees are shaking, I start to scream
I am cold but there is no one to rescue me

My head is cold and my words are trembling
My mouth is dry, oh, I wish I have a cup of coffee
What can I use on my head I say
Tylenol might help but it won't keep me warm

My help, my joy in times of bad days
She warms me up when I look messy
When the day is dull, she brightens my face
And covers the best part of my inner being

I don't know what I can do without you
You have been a joy to me when my day is rough
Oh blessed wig, you make me shine
Thank God I'm blessed, I have my 911 emergency wig

DON'T BITE THE HANDS THAT FED YOU

Once upon a time, I had a friend
Who was more than a friend to me
He took me like his own
Fed, clothe, and had a shelter over my head

Loving me was like an amazement to me
For I was never loved like this before
I was treated like a princess, I worked on red carpets
I stepped on the pillars I had never dreamed of

Calamity took over our love and we fell apart
The wind blew and I still remember
The joy, love, laughter we had shared together
I lost my friend and I lost my love

I regret because I was not there during his critical time
I neglected my love and let him die in vain
Hurts from my pain, I looked the other way
Now it is too late to turn back the clock on my deeds

What can I say to all my friends now
There are people that have been there for you
Through thick or thin, rain or shine, they where there
They are angels, if you neglect them, they will walk away

Whatever the problem is, make amends to solve it
Show remorse, let go of your pride and take your stand
Tomorrow might be too late so think of what I say
You might need that hands again
Don't bite the hands that fed you

THE BALL IS IN YOUR COURT

The ball is in your court how does it bounce
Does it bounce to the left or bounce to the right
Do you kick to quit or kick to continue
Tired of trying when the going gets tough
Expecting it to be better someday

How is the field you are nurturing
Do you work hard in it or sit back to relax
Do you fold your hands and wait to see
What the future holds for you each day
Without doing anything about the problem

My friend, manna does not fall from heaven
Heaven helps those that help themselves
Man has to work hard before he eats in life
Don't give up, keep trying, you will succeed
The ball of life is in your court

GOD MADE YOU FOR A PURPOSE

Can you tell me why God created you
Who knows what he has in store for you
Who can explain the creation of this world
Why where we born and what is our purpose on earth
Nobody knows, that is why it is so amazing

God knows what he was doing when he created you
He created you the way you are without no man's help
He made every one of color, size, shape, and tone
Different culture, personality and with different talents
Loving every day the gifts he has created

Don't forget, you have the fingerprint of God all over you
You are fearfully and wonderfully made
You are the apple of God's eye
You are God's masterpiece
Nothing is awesome, special, unique as you

DON T QUIT ON GOD

Situations may come our way where we need God
In our everyday living that we begin to wonder
Why are things happening to me
Why is every door closing when I go to knock
What have I done to deserve this?

I have asked God but he is still silent
Frustration takes a whole lot of me
Anger melts in and settles in
Never giving in to another word
But the word that says it is time to quit on God

The devil says, "Quit on God, there is no help from them
You have tried but it's time to turn the other way
Turn the other side and look the other way
You will make it but you must leave God's presence
God's presence is not real and it does not exist."

People will fail you but God never fails
They will laugh but God will not laugh at you
God is not deaf, he listens to all that you say
He is not blind, he sees everything that is going on
He cares and he loves you so much

Don't quit on God, oh my friend
You have no other friend to turn to in this world
He is the answer to all your problems
When everything fails, God will never fail
You will have no other friend so why risk a wonderful friend

NOBODY CAN SAY NO

Who is man to say, "You cannot make it"
Is he the giver of life?
Is man the maker of heaven and earth
Who is in control of your destiny?

God answers, "I have formed you in my own image
I am the maker of heaven and earth
I am the breath of life
I have molded you in the palm of my hands

I have created you for a divine purpose
Do not be afraid for I am with you
I will go with you wherever you go"
If God says yes, nobody can say no.

THE WEAPONS OF FIRE

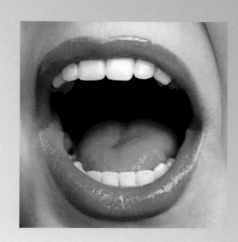

The weapons of fire is in the tongue
Fire could be seen all around it
It could be used as a blessing or cursing
It is a tool that everyone is to be careful

The tool is like a deadly snake
Which crawls all around and looks for something to say
When there is nothing in the mouth
It rules and sweeps from side to side

This vessel is used for spiritual uplifting
Also used for vocal warm-up exercises
All the sweet and bad melodies are heard from the tongue
Which tells us who we really are

Be careful on what you use the vessel to say
For it is deadly, sweet, and bitter
Quick to listen and slow to speak
Watch what you say, it will come back and hunt you
Watch what you say, it will come back and haunt you

JEALOUSY

Jealousy is a bad spirit seen among people
Our friends, loved ones, family members, and coworkers
All around the world, this word can be heard
That sometimes drives us to think at all times
Why is this spirit breaking us apart

Jealousy can make you cruel in a lot of ways
It can make you have unlimited power
Which causes all to lose respect for you
It diminishes your character to a lower level
Which eventually makes things hard and difficult for you

Don't be jealous of what someone else has
If you want it, work hard and go get it
It is not free. It took a lot of time and money
To accomplish the result of today
It took sacrifice.

Jealousy, oh what a bad name
Someone will call and always remember you
Will you like to be classified like this?
Jealousy will bring bitterness and death before your time
Watch out; watch out

MERCY

We often ask for things at a particular time
We cry out for mercy and help
We humble ourselves and look up above
"Lord be merciful, gracious and hearken to my prayers"

As you plead for mercy, how many times do you show mercy
Do you deny people when they ask for mercy from you?
Do you give them a hard time?
Or laugh at their petitions so as to make fun of them?

In every thing we do, we should be merciful
Show mercy to everyone big or small
Break the hardened heart and have a little mercy
Remember someday in this life, you will need mercy again

IT IS NOT OVER

Who has the whole world in his hands?
Who can see the end from the beginning
Who has the power of the highest authority
To speak to the mountains and the mountains obey

The word *it is over is said every day in life*
To scare, challenge, and motivate an individual
How do you feel when you hear this words
How do you react in this situation

Your reaction in life will determine your strength
Whether to give up or move forward
Whatever you do, always remember
It is not over until God says it is over

THANKSGIVING

How often do say thank you
Appreciating what God has done for you
Do you look and say, "If it had not been the Lord
Where would I have been today?"

We all need to be thankful to God every day
For all the bountiful blessings he has bestowed on us all
Through it all, he has been there for us
To see us through our problems whether big or small

Thanksgiving expands the capacity to our blessings
It rebukes depression from our lives
It opens doors to opportunities to our success
And restores what is missing in our lives

DESTINED

You have been programmed to win
You are not here by accident
God has a purpose for you
God has ordained you for such a time like this

You are destined for favor
In everything you do, you will succeed
Victory shall be yours always
Success is set for you for life.

DO YOU USE YOUR TALENTS WISELY

Everyone in this world is blessed with talents
Unique and special that cannot be bought with money
Given freely by God Almighty
For a specific and wonderful purpose

Have you made use of your talent wisely?
Do you make your talent waste without using it
Does it grow to produce fruits?
Is it nurtured and well taken care of?

Be wise, use your talents
You are blessed with great opportunities, wisdom, and knowledge
You are smart in your thinking and endeavors
Bright in all you set your hands to do.

FACE YOUR PROBLEMS

Problems will arise every day in our lives
You can run but you cannot hide from it
Stay calm, pray, God will guide you

Because through him you will get a solution
It will get easier if you face the mountain of your problems

APPRECIATE YOURSELF

Life is full with joys and trials
In every angle, there is joy and happiness
Accomplished by you but we sometimes neglect
To appreciate what we have already conquered

Don't look down at yourself in any way
You have to be thankful for what God had used you to do
Pat yourself on the back and remember you conquered
You achieved and accomplished a goal when you thought you couldn't.

WORRY

Stop worrying about your problems
Problems will always be there
You cannot solve them by worrying
It can be solved through prayers

Prayers can bring you hope in your crises
It can give you insights on handling the problems
Prayers will help you when all things fail
God has the answer so give it all to him.

HOW LONG MUST I WAIT ?

My pains are unbearable, the sores are getting worse
The wound cannot heal and I have been taking medications
Medications are good but I need my healing now
How long must I wait on the Lord?

Problems will bring sorrow and heartaches
That sometimes overwhelm me, that I feel like letting go
I can't take this anymore I want to quit
Patience is the remedy to all our problems

Don't look no further for help, my friend, wait on the Lord
They that wait on the lord shall renew their strength
They will mount up like eagles, they shall run and not be weary
They shall walk and not faint.

STEP OUT OF THE CLOSET

Everyone is birthed with dreams and visions for the future
Dreams that have not been materialized because of fear
Setbacks that have let our visions drain into a pit
Frustration that settles in and kills our dreams

The closet we hide in today is very comfortable
It is safe, easy going, and very enjoyable
Sometimes we feel like getting out but laziness pulls us back
We like our comfort zone so we get so satisfied

To do better in life, we must step out of our comfort zone
People won't understand but who cares of what they think
You have to look for what is best for you in life
Step out of the closet so your dreams will come alive

HOLD ON

Hold on when times are hard
It will get easier along the line
Hold on when there is nothing to hope for
For hope is in the Lord and not in man

FAILURE IS NOT FINAL

Failure comes to bring you down
To bring tears and loss of hope
It glitters as a stream to wipe out joy
That would have been surrounding you every day

It makes us look down at ourselves
Sometimes calls for a pity party
Looking for someone to sympathize
Crawling in every night and day

Wake up; stop looking for consolation all the way
Compose yourself, wipe out frustrations from your face
Go back to the failure road and try again
Nothing is impossible to those who are willing to try

Winners do not quit, you have to try again
Do it again because you will succeed
Recognize that failure is not the end of life
Failure is not final. You can overcome it.

SUNSHINE

A woman of quality and substance
Pretty and well talented
Blessed and well brought up
By her wonderful parents

A lady of real beauty
Who smiles in all troubles
Gathers strength from distress
Grows brave always by reflection and prayers

She came in and presented herself
To the family of Mr. Mbong J. Mbong
Always giving of herself
Without asking for anything in return

Boasting and pride is not her style
She is simple and a very good mother
Spreads her wings and opens her arms
To all who calls and talks to her

You have made me realize one thing
I have a treasure, a sunshine that I would never forget
You have really inspired me
To be the best in everything I do

How can I ever thank you
For all you have done for me
Sunshine, a virtuous woman is who you are
Mrs. Grace K. Mbong

THE VALLEY OF BONES

We all have been through valleys in life
Valleys that have been dried out like bones
Dark days where all we see looks cloudy
Days of hopelessness, difficulties in all ways
No answer, rejection is all that surrounds us

In the valley, our system gets low
We have no place to hide because it is not permanent
We go through tests and trials that won't last
That sometimes looks so difficult to bear
Unfortunately, no one to turn to for relief

Sometimes we have to go through the fire to survive
God sometimes breaks us down so as to raise us up
When we get raised up we are like strong giants
That cannot be defeated
We are God's chosen one

This struggle is painful but we have to be patient
Trouble will not last for a very long time
Don't give up with the bones in your life
God can turn your situation around
If dead bones can live, you will surely live

I WILL SURVIVE

If birds can fly, I will fly again
Troubles will not break me down no more
I will put myself together and spread my wings
And look ahead to see what God has for me

In times of difficulty, look up to the cross
Focus on God for he will answer you
Don't look back or give in
Know that if birds can fly, you will survive

THINK TWICE

Decisions can be made at any time
Sometimes when one is angry, frustrated, and
overwhelmed with joy
That makes the heartbeats be generated fast
Thinking what might be the next step

It is good to make decisions but think again
Do not let your feelings take a whole of you
Take a deep breath, relax, and meditate
You have the final word, think before you act.

SHAKE IT OFF

We have a lot of burdens on our shoulders
Burdens that carry a lot of weight
At times we need a friend to share with
God is your best friend you can hope and rely on

Shake off the spirit of heaviness in you
Put the breastplate of praise in you
Wash off the scales of doubt from your face
Know that God is in control, he will see you through

IN THE MIDST OF THE STORM

When things don't go the way they ought to go
Disappointments, tragedies and setbacks
You look for joy but is nowhere to be found
You seek for help and no one replies

Problems arise as the tension gets high
Confusion becomes the joy of the moment
All doors get closed in every angle you turn to
In the midst of the storm, God is watching over you

God will never leave you nor forsake you
He is a friend closer than a brother
In times of trouble, call on him
For he is the answer to all your problems

SACRIFICE

It takes time and effort
To excel to the top
It looks sometimes weary
When you try to climb the ladder each day

Don't give up on your work
You will reap at the end
To be successful in life
You must sacrifice

SPEAK LIFE

Speak life to yourself
Things will work out for you
Speak with faith and don't doubt
For if you believe, so shall it be.

CREDITS
Photos downloaded from www.sxc.hu

THANKSGIVING : *Photo by Bill Davenport*

DESTINED : *Photo by Martín Orza*

DO YOU USE YOUR TALENTS WISELY : *Photo by Gavin Mills*

FACE YOUR PROBLEMS : *Photo by Jasper Greek Golangco*

APPRECIATE YOURSELF: *Photo by Marcos Santos*

WORRY: *Photo by Kris E. Michel*

HOW LONG MUST I WAIT?: *Photo by Agata Urbaniak (http://www.sxc.hu/profile/straymuse)*

STEP OUT OF THE CLOSET : *Photo by Claudia Meyer*

HOLD ON: *Photo by Radu Andrei Dan*

FAILURE IS NOT FINAL: *Photo by Thad Zajdowicz*

SUNSHINE: *Photo by Thomas Boulvin*

THE VALLEY OF BONES: *Photo by Caroline Gustafsson*

I WILL SURVIVE: *Photo by Nick Goodchild*

THINK TWICE: *Photo by Jolka Igolka*

SHAKE IT OFF: *Photo by Asif Akbar*

IN THE MIDST OF THE STORM: *Photo by Stijn Bossink*

SACRIFICE: *Photo by Roxana Barbulescu*

SPEAK LIFE: *Photo by Salina Hainzl*

Printed in the United States
by Baker & Taylor Publisher Services